THE
Archive Photographs
SERIES

CHADDERTON

This aerial view, c. 1980, shows the area from Whitegate, through Foxdenton and down to Middleton Junction. The most obvious landmark is the cluster of cooling towers at Chadderton Power Station. The station closed and the 'three ugly sisters' were blown up in 1986. This large expanse of land at Slacks Valley is currently being developed as the Broadway Business Park.

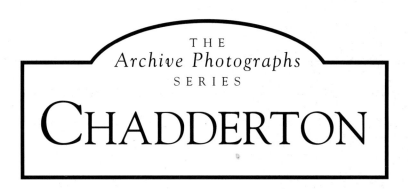

THE
Archive Photographs
SERIES

CHADDERTON

Compiled by
Michael Lawson and Mark Johnson

CHALFORD

The Chalford Publishing Company
St Mary's Mill, Chalford,
Stroud, Gloucestershire, GL6 8NX

ISBN 0 7524 0714 7

Typesetting and origination by
The Chalford Publishing Company
Printed in Great Britain by
Bailey Print, Dursley, Gloucestershire

In memory of Anthony Lawson, twin brother of Michael, a Chaddertonian by upbringing who died whilst this publication was being prepared.

Acknowledgements

Clifford Ashton, Gladys Ashworth, Mary Ashworth, Trevor Ashworth, Denis Barrott, Mary Briggs, British Aerospace (Chadderton), E. Butterworth, Joan Butterworth, Chadderton Chrysanthemum Society, Ena Chadwick, Lily Cheetham, Mrs Crabtree, Mr Dunning, Connie Dyson, May Eastwood, Harold Elly Collection, James Exley, Eunice Garside, Mrs Gartside, Carl Goldberg, Alice Hadfield Collection, Mrs Haughton, Carol Healing, C. Howarth, Mrs Lewis, Kathleen Miller, National Portrait Gallery (London), Margery Ricardo, St Luke's church, St Matthew's church, Mrs Scarsbrook, Charlotte Smith Collection, J. Smith, Jake Tomlinson, Mrs Warburton, Mr M. Warrington and G.F. Wrigley.

A special acknowledgement to the *Oldham Chronicle* for permission to use several photographs from their archives and for their kind support of local history projects.

Attempts have been made to trace the owners of all photographs but the authors wish to apologise for any omissions which may have occurred.

Contents

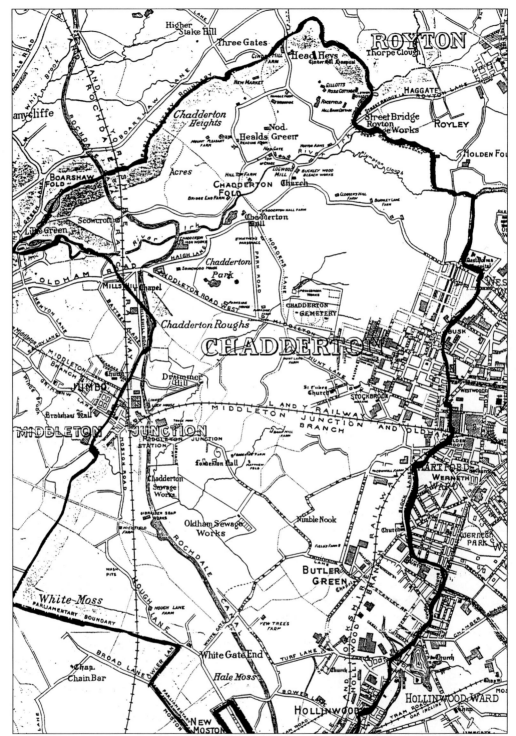

A map of Chadderton in 1900 showing the rural tracts in the west of the town. In the early 1920s Broadway was constructed along a north-south line and was the major factor in the subsequent development of the town.

Introduction

Although it is situated six miles to the north east of the city centre, Chadderton shares a common boundary with Manchester. The town lies in the western foothills of the Pennines, on the edge of the Lancashire coalfield, and is drained by the River Irk and a number of its tributaries. Its name is believed to derive from 'Caderton', a combination of Celtic and Anglo Saxon elements indicating the 'settlement of the hill fort'. The Romans evidently passed through Streetbridge and the ancient township was centred around the Irk in Chadderton Fold, where the manor house, a cluster of cottages and the water powered manorial corn mill stood. The community lived by agriculture, domestic spinning, weaving and other home based trades and crafts. Wool and flax were the original fibres but during the seventeenth century fustian weaving became established and there was also a fulling mill situated on the Irk. Coal mining is first mentioned in the eighteenth century and other early industries included a chemical works and paper manufacture.

For centuries the manorial system added considerable prestige to the township. The first Lord of the Manor of Chadderton and Foxdenton was Geoffrey de Trafford, who came to live here in the early thirteenth century and assumed the name of the estate, becoming Geoffrey de Chadderton. While the early members of the de Chadderton family were notable for their feuds and disputes with neighbours, there were several more peaceable descendants. In 1470 an Edmund Chadderton was appointed Vicar of Kirby Londale, Westmorland, while William Chadderton was consecrated Bishop of Chester in 1579 and in 1595 was translated to Lincoln. Another member of the family, Laurence Chadderton, became the first Master of Emmanuel College, Cambridge, in 1584 and, in 1611, was one of the committee responsible for producing the King James' Bible or Authorised Version.

Families who succeeded to the manor were the Radclyffes, Asshetons and Hortons, whose members achieved fame or formed friendships far beyond the township. John Radclyffe was knighted by King Henry V at the battle of Agincourt in 1415, making him the first of several Lords of Chadderton to receive a knighthood. Thomas Horton was the Governor of the Isle of Man for the Earl of Derby from 1725-1736, while six lords of the manor held the important office of High Sheriff of Lancashire intermittently between 1591 and 1776. During the English Civil War and the Jacobite rebellions, the Radclyffes of Foxdenton were fervent supporters of the Stuart cause, while the last Radclyffe to be born at Foxdenton Hall - Robert in 1737 - became a close friend of the Prince of Wales, later King George III.

The movement for parliamentary reform and for improved working and living conditions for ordinary people had its advocates in Chadderton; in 1801 three Chadderton men were sentenced to seven years transportation to Botany Bay for administering illegal oaths. The township became known for its radicalism. Among the eleven people killed at the Peterloo massacre, two were Chadderton men: John Ashton of Cowhill and Thomas Buckley of Baretrees. Eventually, in 1832, the township was represented in Parliament for the first time when it was included in the Oldham Parliamentary Borough Constituency.

Although Chadderton emerged as a Victorian town dependent predominantly on cotton spinning, its industrial growth was relatively slow. Two water driven cotton mills, the Bank and the Clough, were erected in 1776, but the cotton boom did not really commence until the 1860s. The population of the township in 1790 was about 2,500, in 1801 it was 3,452 and in 1851, still only 6,188. However, its growth between 1861 and 1891 was phenomenal as cotton mills began to cover the area. The population of 7,486 recorded in 1861 had grown to 22,087 in the census of 1891 and the number of mills had increased to thirty-five. By 1901 over 6,000 people were employed in Chadderton's mills and by the start of the First World War the local cotton industry had reached its zenith, with over fifty mills dominating the landscape. Industries ancillary to cotton spinning such as engineering, coal mining, brick making, rope production, bleaching and dyeing, also became prominent during the nineteenth century, whilst a variety of smaller concerns and family firms were much in evidence.

As a result of the rapid growth in population and subsequent urbanisation, Chadderton was changing into an industrial town. Churches, chapels and schools were built and new forms of local government adopted. The town elected its first Local Board of Health in 1873 and, in 1894, became the Urban District of Chadderton, with a council of eighteen members responsible for many social services. A new administrative centre with public buildings and shopping facilities evolved on Middleton Road. By the 1930s, Chadderton was the second largest urban district in Britain's most populous county and its representation on the Lancashire County Council was increased to two members.

Nineteenth century improvements in transport and communications included the Rochdale Canal of 1804, the Middleton to Oldham turnpike road around 1810 and the Lancashire and Yorkshire Railway system. The Manchester to Leeds line through western Chadderton, with a station at Mills Hills, was constructed in 1839 while the branch line to Oldham, with a station at Middleton Junction, followed in 1842. The more direct route from Manchester to Oldham, with a station at Hollinwood in south Chadderton, opened in 1880. This century the central Chadderton branch from the Middleton Junction line opened in 1914, but was for goods only.

From 1902 a tramcar service through the town centre was operated by the Middleton Electric Traction Company and from 1925 by Oldham Corporation, who later shared the responsibility with Manchester, Rochdale and the North Western Company for the local bus services. The arrival of the motor car heralded a new era in road building. In 1925 the arterial road, Broadway, was opened by the Minister of Transport. Its 2.8 miles bisect Chadderton from north to south and it was a major factor in the unification and modernisation ot the town this century. Progress was maintained by the motorway link road from Broadway to the M62 which was opened in 1972. The Chadderton section of the M66 extension is currently being constructed and it is more than likely that Broadway itself will assume the role of a convenient link between these two major motorways.

The accelerating decline in the cotton spinning industry has become an issue this century. Now only two mills, the Chadderton and the Elk (the last mill to be built in Lancashire), still operate in the industry for which they were built. Other industries were established however, notably British Aerospace (originally A.V. Roe), Her Majesty's Stationery Office, whose government printing includes passports, and the former Ferranti electronics division works.

In 1974 Chadderton lost its autonomy when it joined with six other local authorities to form the Metropolitan Borough of Oldham - one of ten new authorities in the newly created County of Greater Manchester. However, its name and 33,000 people live on. With its industrial estates, housing developments, commercial, health, leisure and shopping facilities, its identity is assured as one of the towns which constitute the metropolitan borough.

Michael Lawson BEd, MA

One

Rural Scenes

Until well into the nineteenth century, Chadderton remained a rural township centred on Chadderton Fold. A great period of expansion took place between 1861 and 1891, when the population soared from 7,486 to 22,087 as the cotton industry boomed. However, much of the western part of the town maintained its green appearance until recently, with old lanes and farms dominating the landscape. Since the 1960s a number of new housing estates have been built and these have changed the face of Chadderton beyond recognition. The scenes in this section are a reminder of more pastoral days.

McDougall's chemical works at the side of the Rochdale Canal was for a long time an industrial enclave in the Mills Hill area. This view, from September 1970, changed dramatically when the area was redeveloped as the Irk Vale housing estate.

Viewed from Middleton Road West in May 1973, are the former power station and the Swan and Junction Mills which still exist. The main feature is the vast tract of open land officially known as Chadderton Roughs. Today the Firwood Park Estate, supposedly the largest private development in Europe, occupies the site - but would the houses have sold as readily if the old name had been retained?

Ferney Field Farm in August 1973. This home of the Greenwood family, which was demolished shortly afterwards, was on the road once known as Humphrey Lane. It was also known as 't' Waggon Road' from the days when a tramway conveyed trucks of coal from Hunt Clough to the nearby branch of the Rochdale Canal.

Cragg Cottages, near the River Irk, at Mill Brow, November 1972. These old hand loom weavers' houses were demolished shortly afterwards.

Chadderton Hall Road and its continuation, Burnley Lane, in March 1950. The children are probably coming home from St Matthew's School which is below the church. Note the open fields where Chadderton Hall Junior School and North Chadderton Secondary School now stand.

Chadderton Fold in 1950 showing the Church Inn as the original three storeyed building. The Vale Garage was once a church mission.

Jenkin Hall above Chadderton Fold, in April 1974. The building, which still exists, has a well in its garden and is reputedly linked to other nearby buildings by a secret passage!

A corner of the Chadderton Hall grounds in the 1920s. The two donkeys belonged to the Livsey family who manufactured pickles and preserves at the hall. The sloping path led from the hall to the large lake and it was in this area that the boats were moored.

A scene in Chadderton Hall grounds, *c.* 1915. May Eastwood is riding a horse belonging to the soldiers based at the nearby Chadderton Army Camp.

Nordens Road formed part of the ancient lane which linked Cowhill with Chadderton Fold. This section, at the side of the Hunt Lane Tavern, crosses the Spring Brook by a bridge and ford before going to Chadderton Hall Road. Spring Brook House was part of the Chadwick's industrial hamlet which was demolished on 1985. The site is designated for private housing.

Chadderton Hall Road, *c.* 1907. This road was part of the ancient route from Oldham, through Chadderton, to Middleton and the mother church at Prestwich.

Top Roughs Farm, which was near to Baytree Avenue, being demolished, *c.* 1960.

One of the few farm buildings still remaining in south Chadderton is Owler Lane Farm, which is now partly hidden among twentieth century housing. The farm is believed to date back to 1700.

This view from 1934 is taken from the middle of what is now the extensive Cathedral Road Estate. A more rural scene would be hard to find in Chadderton and St Matthew's church completes the pastoral atmosphere.

A section of Haigh Lane as it was in 1950.

Chadderton Fold, the historic centre of the town, at the turn of the century. The River Irk meanders through the 'fowt' at the side of the Church Inn. Much of this old property has now gone but Jenkins Hall, on higher ground to the right, still remains.

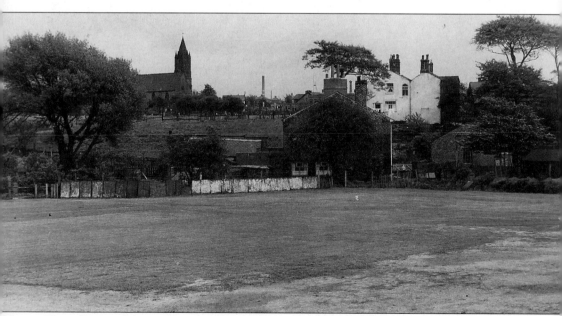

The village cricket pitch at Chadderton Fold in May 1961.

18

The original footbridge over the Rochdale Canal, near the Baytree Mills and Firwood House, as it was in the early years of this century. Under it was the swing bridge for heavier traffic. A new footbridge has recently been erected on the same site.

Seen from Chadderton Park Road around 1950, is the former vicarage of St Matthew's. The wall was part of the old boundary wall which surrounded the Chadderton Hall Estate.

The junction of Broadway and Foxdenton Lane in the 1930s with its quaint street lamps and traffic lights. The garage, left of centre, is now more modern but the Nimble Nook Working Men's Club behind it remains much the same. The former Eaves Lane Co-op, far right, survives today as commercial premises.

Chadderton Park Road early this century. The road leads down to Chadderton Hall which can be seen among the trees to the left. The great barn of Tomlinson's farm survives to this day but the impressive vicarage for St Matthew's church, erected in 1878, was demolished in 1956. The field on the left, now part of the Rydal Avenue estate, housed the Chadderton Army Camp during the First World War.

Two

Seats of Learning

Back in 1606, James Assheton of Chadderton Hall became the co-founder of the grammar school at Oldham, and successive generations of the Chadderton gentry were to be trustees. A school was founded at Healds Green in 1789 and a National School was endowed by Sir Thomas Horton at Cowhill in 1815. After 1870 many new schools were built both by the various churches and the Chadderton School Board. From 1902 the Chadderton Urban District Council had its own education committee and, after the 1944 Act, the town was to be the centre for Lancashire County Council Education Division 23. The variety of photographs in this section recall the 'happiest days of your life'.

Church schools played an important role in the development of education in Chadderton and this class formed part of the Middleton Junction Wesleyan School, *c.* 1900.

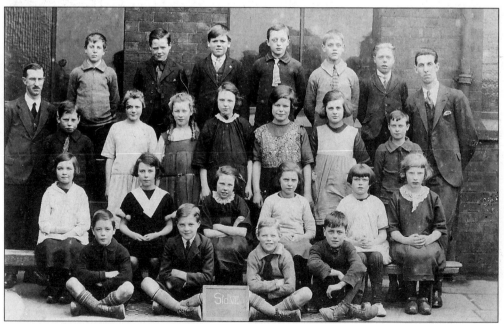

Standard VII at St Luke's School in the early 1930s. The teacher on the right is John Roberts and fourth from the left on the back row is James Sudworth.

Standard V of St Mark's School in 1925. The school, which stood on the corner of Milne Street and Radclyffe Street, was demolished in about 1970 and replaced by the Baretrees Schools.

Class III at St Luke's in the 1940s. Miss Ogden is the teacher and Mr Young the headteacher. Back row, from left to right: Donald Young, Raymond Firth, Travis Seamark, Cyril Johnson, Harry Taylor, Raymond Johnson. Second row: Lily Bertenshaw, Ronald Slater, Eric Blomley, Edmund Slater, Vera Dyson. Front row: Annie Clayton, Eunice Boland, Peggy Beaver, Audrey Turner, Celia Wolstenholme, Margaret Ogden, Irene Goldthorpe.

Masters and boys of North Chadderton School in 1929. Sixth from the left on the back row is Joseph Briggs, a life-long parishioner of St Herbert's RC church and a choir member for nearly seventy years.

Mills Hill School, Baytree Avenue. This class photo dates from the late 1950s or early '60s, when the headteacher, on the left, was Mr Atherton. The school is now the largest in our metropolitan borough with over 600 primary pupils.

The imposing facade of the former Chadderton Grammar School as it was in 1959. Opened in October 1930 by the Earl of Crawford and Balcarres, it was the first co-educational grammar school built by Lancashire County Council. Its aim was 'to provide a thoroughly sound modern education which will fit its pupils for life.'

The staff of Chadderton Grammar School in May 1959, when Mr R. Britton was headteacher. After a long and quite distinguished career as a mixed, and then the boys' grammar school, it became for a short time Mid-Chadderton, and then Radclyffe Secondary School after local government reorganisation in 1974.

A typical, formal classroom in Chadderton Grammar at the time of its opening in October 1930.

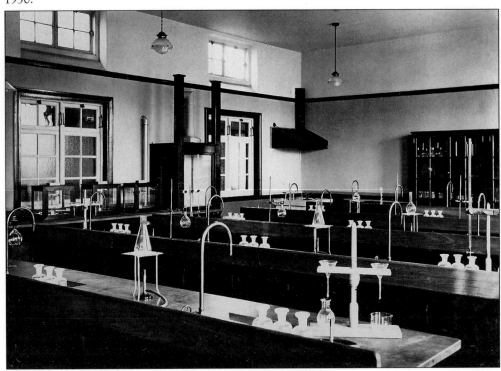

The 'chemical laboratory' at the time of the school's opening.

Three

Our Changing Town Centre

Whilst Chadderton Fold was the historic centre of the township, it was the developments in the later Victorian period which moved the town centre to Middleton Road. Rapid expansion of terrace housing in this area led to the provision of a wide variety of shops on both sides of the road. As local government developed, a town hall, police station, public baths and library were built to become focal points within the town. The following views will evoke nostalgia among residents who remember the vast array of shops which existed until the late 1960s. At the same time it is easy to forget the construction of the many new buildings which occurred in the 1970s.

William Moores and his wife outside their barbers shop in 1898. The shop, at No. 386 Middleton Road, was opposite the present Springfield Garage and besides selling tobacco also repaired umbrellas!

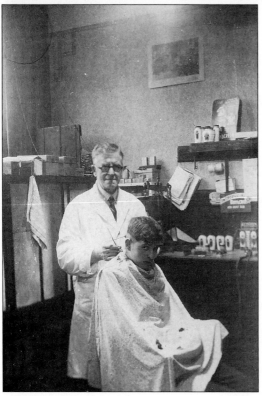

Fifty years later and son, Harry Moores, carries on the same trade. This interior is typical of a barbers shop in the early 1950s.

Middleton Road, *c.* 1910, with a tramcar of the Middleton Electric Traction Company reaching its terminus at the Oldham boundary. Lansdowne Road is to the right but Walton Street, on the left, has now disappeared.

Looking up Middleton Road past the Springfield Garage in June 1963. The Granada Red Arrow shop in the centre carried the name stone 'Chadderon Bazaar'. The white gabled building further up the row was the Free Trade public house which closed down in June 1972.

Shops near the baths as they were in 1965. Apart from public buildings, only the Sun Mill Inn remains.

Brown's Stores, c. 1947, was two shops separated by Croft's fish shop. Brown's eventually merged all three shops and even had a cafe upstairs.

The Rose Queen, Sheila Blomley from St Luke's church, passes the old Co-op stores in 1952. The shop on the right was the drapers and next door was the hardware store. The door on the far left led upstairs to the Co-op reading and newsroom. The site is now the landscaped area in front of the Asda petrol station.

This unusual view of 1963 from the balcony of the town hall, recalls shops such as Simmons' Electrical and the North Western Gas showroom.

Familiar, and yet not quite so familiar! The library in the early 1930s still had its ornate wall around it and a dome above the entrance, although the flagpole had gone. The original baths had a few years of life left before demolition and tramcars rattled through the town centre.

Thirty years later and the new baths have long been established, the library has lost its dome and wall, and cars are becoming increasingly popular. However, this photograph seems to have captured a particularly quiet time of day!

Chadderton was proud to proclaim its identity back in 1962. From Lansdowne Road, this scene shows Anderton's chemist at the corner of Walton Street.

For better or for worse, urban renewal has arrived and large tracts of old Busk were demolished by the late 1960s. The Horton Arms public house is still with us and the Yorkshire Bank moved into the new precinct, but Miss Masters of Chadderton was one of the many retail outlets which were unfortunately lost. The buildings next to the garage housed the surgery for one local group of GPs.

The old Yorkshire Bank at the corner of Ward Street and Middleton Road. The fashions proclaim the early 1970s, and the demolition of the Busk area allows an uninterrupted view of the town hall after its facelift.

The building in the foreground was a doctor's surgery; next door was the local branch of the National Westminster Bank which declined taking up a unit in the new precinct. The imposing bulk of the Melbourne Mill, which at this time manufactured Pakamac rainwear, looms in the distance. This view was taken from the corner of Garforth Street around 1970.

The next three photographs from the early 1970s, form a series which examines the south side of Middleton Road, from the town hall down to Milne Street.

This block was directly opposite the library. Butterworth's butchers, the post office and Travis' jewellers, all relocated in the precinct.

Only the baths and the Sun Mill Inn still exist in this scene, taken from outside the Co-operative store which stood on the site of the Asda petrol station.

Demolition of the town centre is well under way by 1971 and the Spinners' Arms and the whole range of Co-op shops have disappeared forever.

The site of the Wren Mill was cleared in 1970 in readiness for the first Asda superstore. The Spring Vale Mill in the background was later to provide extra parking spaces.

The old and the new co-exist in this redevelopment scene from February 1974. The first phase of the Asda superstore has been completed and the extension has commenced. To the left the new Reform Club has opened while, further up the picture, the original version of the new precinct is beginning to take shape. The Rushbank and Spring Vale Mills can still be seen with the Spring Vale public house, known locally as the 'Khartoum', showing at the top.

Building work on the new shopping centre, seen from behind the Reform Club, proceeds rapidly in 1974. The Melbourne Mill, a relic of Chadderton's Victorian past, was finally demolished in 1980 and the site incorporated into the redevelopment area.

Looking into the new precinct in 1974, a year before its opening. The Asda store opened in 1972 but an extension, seen on the right, was then constructed.

Four
Leisure and Pleasure

All work and no play... In the following photographs the social activities of the people of Chadderton are documented. Sporting events of various kinds have been recorded from school teams and church teams to the successes of clubs. Outings of different kinds were popular, whilst amateur dramatics also find a place in the recreational pursuits of Chaddertonians.

Part of the pleasure gardens at Chadderton Hall at the turn of the century. Thousands of people came to spend the day admiring the wide variety of animals which were exhibited there by the entrepreneur, Joseph Ball.

The pleasure gardens made use of the large lake which lay in the grounds of Chadderton Hall. Boating came to an impromptu halt in 1927 when a violent rainstorm caused floods which, among other damage, breached the lake. Unfortunately it was never reinstated.

Members of St Herbert's RC church
splendidly arrayed for a fancy dress ball in
1919.

A children's sports day, sometime in the
1930s. After their religious processions at
Whitsuntide, most churches held a 'Field
Day' at a local venue. This is the Albert
Taylor Memorial Ground behind
Foxdenton Park. The hall can be seen to
the right and the great barn, demolished
only a few years ago, is much in evidence.

Washbrook Primitive Methodist Football Club. Judging by the cup in front of them the players certainly have something to celebrate at the end of the 1929/30 season.

A relaxing game of putting at Foxdenton Park in the late 1920s. The green was near the main entrance to the park and is now covered by the tennis courts.

The Cow and Calf public house was at the side of the canal at Foxdenton Lane; it closed in 1933 when in the tenancy of Clare Haugh. This group of men, mainly in flat caps and sporting flowers, seem ready for an enjoyable day's outing during the late 1920s.

The basket ball team at Butler Green Mission in the 1920s. The mission was a branch of Christ church and was established in 1885.

Chadderton and District Band outside the town hall in 1952. Judging by the trophies, they had apparently had a very successful season. The band had its origins back in the eighteenth century and is still going strong.

Pride and Prejudice performed by the pupils of Chadderton Grammar School during the 1950s. The gentleman third from the left is John Grisedale, whose cousins, the Howitts, ran the printing firm in the old town hall.

Preparing to bowl the first 'wood' on the green at Nimble Nook Working Men's Club. Unfortunately little is known about the bowlers in this 1930s scene but they were presumably club officials.

Broadway may be heavily congested today but this scene recalls the far quieter days of the 1930s. This horse and trap have just passed Chadderton Grammar School (now Radclyffe Lower) journeying towards Middleton Road.

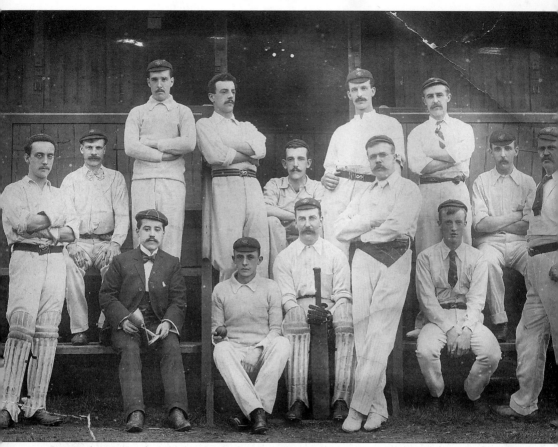

St Matthew's Cricket Club, also known as Chadderton Park Cricket Club, early this century. Back row, from left to right: Bob Lord, David Bell, Tom Buckley (whose father was the registrar at Chadderton Cemetery), -?-, -?-, Charlie Whitehead, -?-, -?-, Bracewel Wrigley, Harry Berry, John Starkey. Front row, seated: Tommy Knott (whose family owned Chadderton ropewalk), Luke Noton, -?-, -?-, George Herbert Wrigley, Ben Dyson.

Pleasant sunshine is the order of the day as these 'regulars' of the Sportsman's Arms, at the junction of Denton Lane and Broadway, prepare for a day's outing in about 1930. The white haired gentleman in the doorway is Alfred Elly. The original inn, one of Chadderton's earliest, dates back to around 1794 and in its time has also been known as the Green Man and the Gamekeepers Arms!

The tennis team at Chadderton Grammar School in about 1955, when it was still a mixed school. On the right is Joan Wilde (now Butterworth).

The opening of the bowling green at North Chadderton Social Club was done in style back in June 1937. Guest of honour was Major Charles Robert Eustace Radclyffe, the lord of the manor, who is seen to the left of the Chairman of the Chadderton Urban District Council, Thomas Hilton.

St Luke's soccer team pose as champions of the Middleton League in the 1921/22 season.

Known as 'Britain's greatest-ever amateur swimmer', Henry Taylor died in Chadderton in 1951 at the age 65. His career spanned half a century and he won numerous trophies, including four Olympic gold medals.

These cadets, attached to Emmanuel parish church and looking extremely proud, pose for the camera, *c.* 1917.

Denton Lane School Football Club. In the 1934/35 season they were the winners of the League and Challenge Cup for the fifth successive year. They also won the Daily Dispatch Shield and the Oldham Athletic Challenge Cup.

A charabanc, typical of the 1920s and early '30s, prepares to take its patrons for a day trip away from the industrial grime. The scene is outside the Nimble Nook Working Men's Club on Foxdenton Lane.

Bowling on the green at Chadderton Hall, *c.* 1920. The man on the left is James Livsey, who operated the pickle factory at the hall and to the right is James Fitton, a veteran councillor for Chadderton, whose name is commemorated in Fitton Park, opposite the Rifle Range public house. The other figures include members of the Livsey and Eastwood families, who were inter-related.

St Herbert's church football team, *c.* 1920. Their Irish connections are obvious!

Mr H. Fowden leads the Rochdale Hounds from the Church Inn at Chadderton Fold, in December 1954. The muddy ground of that time has now become a well kept, official village green.

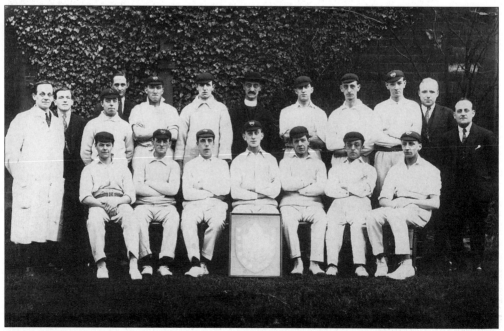

The football team at St Luke's church were the proud winners of the Middleton League Second Division in 1921. The vicar at the time was Mr Hayes.

52

Judging the exhibits at the Chadderton Chrysanthemum Society's twenty-third annual show held in the town hall in 1963. The society, which is still in existence, dates back to 1938.

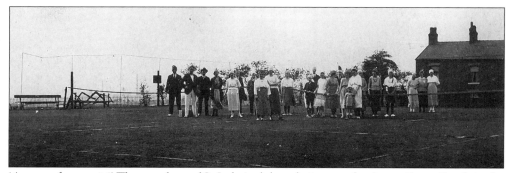

'Anyone for tennis?' The members of St Luke's club at their ground at James Street South in the 1930s.

With a cup to prove it, the bowling team at St Herbert's church end a successful season in the mid 1950s. Holding the cup is Bill Naylor and on his right is Leonard Gallagher. Standing between them is Joe Marsh, while on the far left is Gerard Keeley.

In March 1935 the junior hockey team of Chadderton Grammar School became the Champions of the Junior Lancashire League. Back row, from left to right: E. Buckley, M. Butterworth, C. Dyson, M. Ashton, M. Fisher, M. Booth, Miss Brown. Front row: E. Bentley, M. Butters, E. Elson, M. Bradbury, J. Hobson.

Five
Out of the Ordinary

A small collection of photographs forms this section. All are concerned with aspects of accidents or disasters of different kinds which, to the people present at the time, would have long remained in their minds. A number of the events took place within the last forty-five years and there will be many people still around for whom these pictures will recall half forgotten memories.

Workmen clearing the culvert which channelled the River Irk under the railway embankment at Mills Hill. The blockage was caused by the debris brought down the river by the floodwater which resulted from the torrential downpour of 11 July 1927.

The torrential rain caused the Rochdale Canal to burst its banks at the aqueduct over the River Irk and the water cascaded into the river below. The empty canal was obviously a source of interest to the locals. The buildings and chimneys belonged to McDougall's chemical works where, during the Second World War, a 'top secret' powder was made that kept the Forces free from typhus-carrying lice!

The extent of the damage to the Irk aqueduct and canal can be seen in this view of 14 July 1927.

By 24 July a wooden trough had been constructed to enable the water in the canal to flow again while the aqueduct was repaired. In the background are the Duke of Bridgewater public house, the cottages at Turnings, the golf house at Little Acres and Lower Acres Farm. Much of this property has since been demolished.

'Chadderton Pier'. Our pier may not be as well known as that at Wigan, but here is the proof of its existence as people take a stroll on it, and under it, while the tide is out! McDougall's chemical works, seen at the left, used the jetty when loading barges with their goods. Fortunately the damage to the canal after the flood was soon repaired.

The floods which occurred in August 1931, at Coalshaw Green. This area, at the junction of Turf Lane, was prone to flooding. The shops to the right are still in existence.

A serious accident at the top of Foxdenton Lane in the 1930s. Note the traffic lights at the Broadway junction.

An accident on Broadway in the 1940s leaves sacks of coal from the lorry involved in the collision, hanging from the doors of this car. The houses in the background place the scene at the top of Foxdenton Lane.

A spark from a flue in the roof was responsible for the destruction of the roof of St Luke's church during the morning of 11 February 1954. Considerable damage was done to the church by the smoke and water. The Rededication Service was held on 30 April 1955.

It took days to dampen down the smouldering bales of cotton after the fire which totally destroyed one half of the Textile Mill on Cobden Street. The fire broke out early in the evening of 11 July 1950 and over 200 firemen with 25 water jets were needed to tackle the blaze. The half which survived was afterwards used for a variety of purposes and was only demolished in 1995.

An Oldham Corporation No. 3 bus going down to Mills Hill, and a Rochdale Corporation No. 90 express travelling from Manchester, collided at the Middleton Road and Broadway junction in the early evening of 1 May 1951. The junction is now wider but little has changed on the Middleton side except for the houses next to the cemetery, which were demolished in the 1960s. St Herbert's School now occupies the site behind the Turog shop, now Delwyn Jebbs photographers.

The Rochdale bus was thrown over and forty-three people were rushed to hospital, though fortunately none were seriously injured. The row of houses still exists and what is now Snippers was then a sweet shop, which served as a first aid centre on the night of the accident.

Six
Trade and Industry

The earliest cotton mills in Chadderton, both water powered, were the Clough and the Bank, built around 1776. The ruins of the latter may still be seen in the fields near Crossley Bridge, Broadway. As industrialisation advanced, mills began to cover the landscape and Chadderton had no fewer than fifty-five of these giants. The great majority have now vanished and of those that remain, only the Elk and the Chadderton still process cotton. Although cotton was the dominant industry there were also several coal mines and other trades ancillary to the production of the fabric. It should also be remembered that agriculture did not die out completely; haymaking and the raising of sheep and cattle are still carried out in the area as they have been for centuries.

Canal barges iced in near the Duke of Bridgewater public house, Mills Hill, in 1905. The canal, opened in 1804, was closed to through navigation after the Second World War whilst the inn was demolished in 1956. The bridge at Walk Mill lock still remains and there are plans to fully restore and reopen the waterway by the year 2004 - its bicentenary.

The lift bridge over the canal at Foxdenton Lane. This was erected in 1928 to replace a swing bridge and was removed in 1972. A new lift bridge is now planned as part of the restoration scheme. The railway was opened in 1839 by George Stephenson and is one of the two main cross-Pennine routes from Manchester. The Railway and Linnet public house on the right dates back to around 1800; across the road the former Co-op store was demolished in the 1970s.

Without doubt our greatest asset is British Aerospace. We are proud to have it within our boundaries and the firm has been equally proud to proclaim its Chadderton connection! Opened just before the last war as A.V. Roe, it produced more than 40 per cent of the total wartime output of Avro Lancaster bombers. The fuselage assembly section is seen here after a serious fire in October 1960.

The Textile Mill, opposite the baths, was built in 1882 and equipped with Platt's machinery as a 'show' mill to which potential customers were brought. It had a chequered career, was half destroyed by fire in 1950, and then completely demolished in 1995. Its dignified tower symbolised an earlier period when 'cotton was king'!

Management and overlookers at the Sun Mill in August 1910. The mill, built in 1861 and demolished in 1986, was one of the largest ever built. Back row, from left to right: J. Hibbotson, T. Jobson, F. Dawson, E. Swindells, J. Rigby. Middle row: J. Russell, T. Mellor, W. O'Neill, R. Thompson. Front row: W. Baker, J. Hyde, A. Neild, J. Barnes, J. Ashton, L. Fletcher.

The directors and senior management of the Sun Mill early this century. Billy O'Neill, to the right of the table, was to be the manager for many years. Founded as a workers' co-operative the mill was the first limited liability company in Lancashire.

The workers and monumental mason's yard of Edward Butterworth in 1907. Founded in about 1880, the premises stood at No. 589 Middleton Road, between the original junction of Dalton Street and the Cemetery Inn, now the Harlequin.

Butterworth's yard closed in about 1965, but a similar yard still operates opposite the cemetery gates and a third once existed at the top of Hamilton Street.

James Chadwick's calico print works, at Springbrook off Middleton Road, early this century. Established in 1875, the firm closed in the early 1980s. The extensive Chadderton Cemetery had an Anglican chapel (now demolished) in the centre, and a Non-conformist one to the right. The Spring Vale Mill to the left and the many chimneys in the background, testify to the strength of the local cotton industry.

Bower Colliery, south Chadderton, in 1913. Coal mining in the town goes back centuries and the Bower was the last pit to close down in the 1920s.

John Smith, the colliery manager at the Bower, is seen to the right of the sign 'Bower colliery, working pit pony'.

A rare view taken underground shows the dangers associated with the mining industry. The grim reality may be sensed by the lamps and pit props. John Smith, manager, is on the right, whilst his colleague is believed to be Mr Marland.

Two pit boys return to the surface at the Bower Colliery at the end of their shift, each carrying the all-important safety lamp. The boy on the left is believed to be called Collinson.

Mechanisation was the focal point of the Industrial Revolution. This photograph of the engine and winding gear at the Bower Colliery dates from the 1920s.

The powerful steam engine at the Magnet Mill, Denton Lane, was built by George Saxon of Manchester and could achieve 1,700 hp. It would drive all the cotton bale breaking and cleaning machinery, the carding engines and preparatory machines, all the spinning frames which comprised 60,156 mule spindles, 44,680 ring spindles and, finally, the cone winding frames. The mill was demolished in the late 1960s and the site is now occupied by the Fold Green Estate.

A number of farms still exist in Chadderton, mainly in the North Ward. This scene in the Central Ward in the early 1950s shows Fred Sherratt taking the first cut in front of No. 482 Kensington Avenue. Mary Sudworth passes the time of day with him.

Making hay at Top Roughs Farm, now covered by the Firwood Park Estate, c. 1951. George Sherratt is driving the tractor whilst his brother Fred supervises the operation. The boys are Fred Sudworth and Peter Stanley.

Left: Mr Gorry, the manager at Chadderton Power Station in October 1983, just after the station had been taken out of use. Right: Part of a control panel at the power station after the shut down.

Chadderton 'B' station opened in 1955 to replace a smaller station. Its three cooling towers and two chimneys - each of which was 365 ft high - were a landmark both from a distance and from the air. The station became redundant in 1982 and was demolished in 1986. This dramatic picture shows the first cooling tower being blown up in April of that year.

Part of central Chadderton viewed from a tower block at Cowhill, in August 1974. The mills, from left to right, are the Stockfield, Melbourne, Textile (or half of it!) and the Sun. Only the first mill remains. In the foreground on the left can be seen the storage yard of Partington's builders which covers the site of the former Palm Mill. On the other side of Stock Lane were the Forge and Vale Mills. On the skyline can be seen the Elk, Fernhurst, Manor and Kent Mills.

Seven
Celebration and Demonstration

A contingent from the township marched to Manchester in 1819 to demonstrate for civil rights. They were to be caught up in the Peterloo massacre and two of their number were killed. The need to march with bands and banners, to celebrate and demonstrate with gatherings and displays, is basic to us all. These photographs reflect the times when Chadderton people have met socially, whether for religious or political reasons, a wedding, to join in public rejoicing, or just for fun!

A political demonstration in about 1910 pauses at the bottom of Coalshaw Green Road. It is believed to be a gathering of the Independent Labour Party which put forward two candidates in Chadderton South Ward as early as the first election for the urban district council in 1894.

Whitegate Lane, near its junction with the Ace Mill. The residents celebrate the end of the First World War in fitting style.

St Luke's Whit Walk early this century, as it turned from Hunt Lane into a cobbled Queens Road. All the terraced property, together with the Melbourne Mill in the left background, has now gone but the Stockfield Mill to the right is still with us. The end house on the right was next to Dairy Street and was for many years, Mrs Pott's Chippy.

The Church Lads' Brigade at St Luke's stands to attention alongside members of the King's Royal Rifles. The photograph, from around 1924, was taken at the top of Queens Road.

The date is 8 April 1914 and within four months the peace and calm would be shattered by the outbreak of the First World War. Herbert Wrigley, who lived at Albion House, and his bride Ann Wolstencroft, who lived at Buckley Wood, Streetbridge, were married at St Matthew's church and then held their reception at Chadderton Hall. This former home of the manorial

lords was gradually becoming derelict and the whole scene undoubtedly speaks of a vanishing era. Next but one to the bride is George Herbert Wrigley, the groom's father and a Chadderton councillor. His two younger sons are on the far left, Gerald at the front and Reginald, who is still living, behind him.

This row of houses on Middleton Road was demolished in the early 1970s and is now occupied by the St Herbert's Court development for the elderly. The bay fronted houses to the left survived until the '80s and were replaced in recent years by the Good Night Inn and Mrs Muffin's Food Emporium.

The visit of King George V and Queen Mary in July 1913 called for a display of loyalty, as shown in both these scenes. This row of houses still exists on Middleton Road opposite the cemetery wall; the decorated homes were Nos 773 to 779.

Members of St Luke's church, led by an impressive band, march to the town hall for a Whitsuntide joint service. The scene is at the junction of Middleton Road and Broadway in the 1930s.

Members of Christ church make their procession of witness along Fields New Road in the 1930s. The tower of the Mona Mill can be seen above the centre, but many of the mills which once lay alongside this road have now gone.

The Rose Queen of St Saviour's church processes to the end of Denton Lane, *c.* 1951. This 'tin' church was replaced in the 1960s by a modern church, but structural faults meant that it was abandoned. The present church is sited near the junction of Denton Lane and Fields New Road.

Led by their scout band the members of Mills Hill Baptist church march down Middleton Road West in about 1957. The drummer to the right is Herbert Taylor and in front of the flag is Fred Sudworth, the scout leader.

The children of St. Luke's School celebrating Empire Day, probably in 1940. The teacher is Mrs Holt who lived in Butterworth Street. Wartime measures are evident by the boxes, containing gas masks, which all children had to carry.

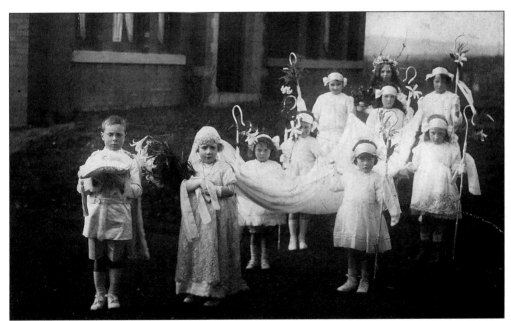

A May Procession at St Herbert's RC church in 1922. The May Queen is Doris Riley and the cushion bearer is Edward Kilgannon. Among the retinue are Ann Brennan, Joan Anderson, Evelyn Coggeran, May Horner, Kathleen Horner and Mary Briggs.

Alice and Billy Hall celebrating their Silver Wedding Anniversary at the town hall, *c.* 1951. They owned a shop in Charles Street but all this area of old Busk has now gone.

Mills Hill School fancy dress competition, *c.* 1959. James Sudworth is the pirate on the right.

Eight
O Praise Ye the Lord

Until 1844 Chadderton was part of the large parish of Prestwich-cum-Oldham with no church of its own. St Matthew's Parish was formed at that time and subsequently, four other Anglican parishes and a number of daughter and mission churches served the town. Non-conformity was also very strong in the area and many Methodist churches were built, along with those for Baptists and Congregationalists. The Roman Catholic church is represented by two places of worship, whilst a Salvation Army hall and several Gospel halls once existed. The spiritual dimension to life is recalled in the following material.

The interior of Chadderton church - St Matthew's - in 1910, showing the gas lamps which were in use from 1894 to 1922. Before their installation services could not be held after 3.00 pm. Inset is the Revd S. Weeks, the vicar there for thirty-eight years.

The manse for Mills Hill Baptist church, as it was in August 1975.

The Revd S. Weeks around the turn of the century in his study at the former vicarage. This stood on Nordens Lane and was demolished in 1958. He was the vicar at Chadderton church from 1873 to 1911, during which time he conducted 1,907 baptisms, 3,113 marriages and 5,797 funerals! This scene captures the atmosphere of a late Victorian or Edwardian room.

Block Lane, one of the oldest roads in Chadderton, in 1905. A window cleaner is at work on one of the bay windows of the impressive Christ Church vicarage. The house, built in the 1870s, was demolished in the 1960s.

St Saviour's Mission church, c. 1910. A daughter church of Christ Church, it stood at the bottom of Denton Lane but was replaced in the 1960s by a modern building which soon developed structural problems and was sold as offices. To the right is Denton Lane School, now demolished, but it had over 300 pupils in the first decade of this century.

Chadderton P.S.A. Mission Hall.

Chadderton P.S.A. (Pleasant Sunday Afternoon) and Working Men's Mission was founded in 1903, and the church building erected in 1910. The street at its side was known as Board Street because it contained the public yard of the Chadderton Local Board. After the demolition of terraced property in the early 1970s it was renamed Apfel Lane. The P.S.A. closed about fifty years ago, but the building remains in light industrial use.

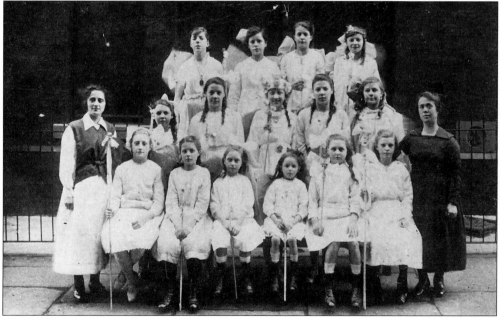

This group outside the P.S.A. mission seem to be commemorating some special event with the girl in the centre suitably crowned. The two ladies are thought to be sisters who lived in Butterworth Street.

Father James Lawless, who was the curate at Corpus Christi RC church, south Chadderton, early this century. In 1916 he was made rector of the new parish of St Herbert's and celebrated the first Mass in the Conservative Club on Victoria Street on 1 July, the day the Battle of the Somme commenced. He left Chadderton in 1924.

The interior of the present Corpus Christi RC church at its opening in 1933. The parish was founded in 1878 and a combined school and church was opened in 1904. At one period the parish was served by no less than three priests.

St Luke's parish church in April 1924, when the Revd J. Hayes was vicar. The church was built in 1888 but the proposed tower and spire extending to 57 metres was never erected. Although not the official parish church, its central position in the town gave it a special role whenever civic services were held by the urban district council.

The choir at St Luke's, *c.* 1947. The organist was Mr Strickland and the choirmaster, Mr Ormerod. Seventh from the right on the back row is Tom Jones, and on the far right is Rowland Ellis.

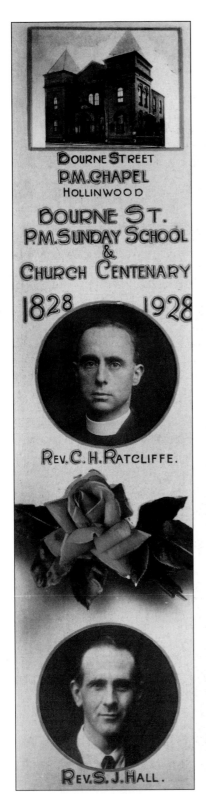

BOURNE STREET
P.M.CHAPEL
HOLLINWOOD

BOURNE ST.
P.M.SUNDAY SCHOOL
&
CHURCH CENTENARY

1828   1928

REV. C. H. RATCLIFFE.

REV. S. J. HALL.

Bourne Street Primitive Methodist church, on the
southern boundary of Chadderton, was one of the first
Methodist churches in the town, being founded in 1828.
Like many similar places of worship it no longer exists.
This bookmark commemorates its centenary and features
the superintendent and the second minister. An old
scholar and official was Walter Brierley, who was
Chairman of the Chadderton UDC in 1922-23, and who
gave his name to the bridge which carried the newly-
constructed Broadway over the Rochdale Canal at the
Boat and Horses.

Bourne Street Primitive Methodist church.

The schoolroom at Bourne Street Primitive Methodist church. Both Bourne and nearby Clowes Street, took their names from early pioneers in the Methodist movement.

A youthful Father George Tighe with Sunday school organiser, Sister Bonaventure and May Queen, Winifred Hampshire, outside St Herbert's presbytery, c. 1930. Canon Tighe, as he was later to become, was the parish priest from 1924 until 1975. Winifred's father had a plumbers shop on Middleton Road.

Although founded in 1916, St Herbert's RC Parish used a temporary 'tin' church for the first forty years. On Saturday 7 July 1956, the foundation stone of the present church was laid by the Bishop of Salford, Dr Beck, who was surprised to see that the roof timbers were already in position. From left to right, leading the procession, are altar servers Terence Marsh, Paul Bowers and Gerard Gallagher.

Washbrook Primitive Methodist church was opened in 1893 to replace the smaller building of 1868, which is to the left. The clock tower was erected by public subscription. All these buildings were demolished around 1969.

Two chapels stood in Chadderton Cemetery, one for Anglicans and one for Non-conformists. The former, seen in 1974, has now been demolished and the other is only used for storage purposes.

Eaves Lane Methodist chapel in 1907. Members first met in a cottage in nearby Thompson Lane in 1903, and one of their first preachers, Robert Cooper, was known as the 'Bishop of Eaves Lane'. The church closed around 1969 when five local churches joined together to build the new South Chadderton Methodist church.

Demolition work in progress in 1984 on the Middleton Road Primitive Methodist church. Sadly, a great number of churches and chapels have now vanished from Chadderton, their presence being marked only in the record books and by their influence on countless generations. This church, which stood opposite Milne Street, was erected in 1869 and the adjacent Sunday school extended in 1898.

Nine

Manorial and Civic

The first lord of the manor, Geoffrey de Chadderton, came to rule his inheritance in the first half of the thirteenth century. Although the halls at Chadderton and Foxdenton changed hands several times during subsequent centuries, the manorial history of Chadderton constitutes a most important period of development. The manorial system lasted well into modern times when it was succeeded by a more democratic form of government in which the town hall, and not the manor house, became central to the lives of the people of Chadderton. Aspects of both forms of administration are considered in this chapter.

The portrait of Sir Watts Horton by the Lancashire artist, Romney. Sir Watts was Lord of the Manor of Chadderton from 1774 until his death in 1811. During this time Chadderton Hall was at its most magnificent, being very tastefully furnished. The grounds were carefully laid out and members of the country gentry attended such social functions as *fêtes champetre* and archery contests. Sir Watts, who was High Sheriff of Lancashire in 1775, was well respected by all and was known as 'a poor man's friend and a good neighbour'.

Chadderton Hall, *c.* 1920, with 'Freehold Dwelling House' and 'Sale by Auction' notices on the gatepost. To the left are the turnstiles through which thousands of visitors entered at the turn of the century to visit Joseph Ball's menagerie, boating lake and pleasure gardens. This ancestral manor house, the origins of which went back to the thirteenth century, was finally to become a pickle factory before being demolished in 1939.

The south front of Foxdenton Hall, *c.* 1930. The hall was rebuilt in 1700 but this view shows the Victorian sash windows and sills which were removed in the major restoration of 1962-65.

Foxdenton Hall, Foxdenton Park.

Foxdenton Park on a summer's day in the 1920s, with the ice cream cycle clearly in evidence. The hall, however, is well on its way to dereliction and is but a shadow of its former glory. This home of the Radclyffes, joint lords of the manor, dates back to about 1454 but was rebuilt in 1620 and again in 1700.

Foxdenton Hall
Foxdenton Park. Middleton Junction. 9.

The north front of Foxdenton Hall as it was in the mid 1930s. The hall was leased to the Chadderton UDC in 1922 by the Radclyffe family and in 1960 it became the council's property.

The official coat of arms granted to the Chadderton Urban District Council in September 1955. Before that date an unofficial insignia had been in use since the early days of the UDC. The arms denote the manorial descent of the town showing two griffins - half eagle, half lion - representing the Trafford and Chadderton families, the central spur rowel of the Asshetons, and the two diagonal black bendlets of the Radclyffes. Two red roses are a reminder of the town's links with the historic county of Lancaster. The crest symbolises the local industries with the anvil for engineering, the eagle for aircraft manufacture, and the shuttle for the former cotton industry.

Chadderton's second town hall opened in 1913 as 'a broad and strong treatment of the English Renaissance'. It occupies the site of Belton Place which had been occupied by mill owners' homes, probably similar to the adjacent Rushbank houses. This scene was probably captured shortly after its opening.

A formal study of Inspector Thomas Huggins, who was in charge of the Lancashire Constabulary police station in Chadderton from 1902 to 1913. At that time he actually lived on the premises in one of the houses that was part of the building. The new station was opened in 1901 to replace the earlier one of 1875, and in 1994 it was totally restructured and refurbished.

Chadderton's first town hall was the former Lyceum building which was erected in 1868 and taken over by the Local Board about 1874. It stood on the corner of Melbourne Street and Middleton Road, opposite Kwiksave, and after the present town hall was opened was used for a number of purposes including a printers, a cafe, and a glass merchants. This view dates from April 1972, three years before the building was demolished.

The original swimming baths were sanctioned by the Chadderton Local Board but were opened in 1894 by the urban district council. They closed in 1935 and the present baths opened on the same site two years later.

As part of the celebrations for the Silver Jubilee of King George V and Queen Mary, the town hall was floodlit and illuminated. Until local government reorganisation in 1974, the facade, balcony and dome of the building were floodlit each Christmas as part of the seasonal festivities.

Chadderton Town Hall.

507.

The town hall, c. 1920, as seen from Springfield House, now occupied by Springfield Garage. The house on the right was Hardcroft, which was demolished in about 1970. The houses to the left, Rushbank, are still in existence. All these large houses were built for local mill owners in the middle of the nineteenth century.

The men who determined the destiny of our town back in 1937. This impressive gathering outside the town hall is presumably the entire urban district council of eighteen members, plus others. The Chairman of Chadderton Council in that year was Thomas Hilton and on his left is the Clerk to the Council, J. Schofield.

104

Part of the council chamber in the town hall, in January 1974, just two months before its function ended under local government reorganisation. On 31 March centuries of local autonomy, culminating in the Chadderton Urban District Council, came to an end. The town hall keeper is Mr Nuttall.

Left: Cemeteries which contain the dead of the First World War have an official memorial. This cross is on the corner of the main walk as you enter Chadderton Cemetery. Right: Before an assembly of over 7,000 people, the Chadderton War Memorial was opened on 8 October 1921 by Councillor Ernest Kempsey. The figure is by Toft of London. This photograph is presumably from the late 1920s.

Posing on the staircase of the town hall in 1939 are these members of the Lancashire County Council, Air Raid Precaution team, based at the control centre in Chadderton. The team were, back row, from left to right: J.S. Cox, P. Eckersley, P. Braddock. Fourth row: Mrs N. Dickenson, Miss F. Esker, Miss V. Berry, Miss A. Ogden. Third row: Miss E. Lowe, Miss K. Hartley, Mrs J.S. Cox, Capt H. Brabin JP (controller). Second row: Miss V. Jackson, Miss P. Rodgers. Front row: Mrs H. Brabin, Miss M. Oldham, Mrs J. Wilde CC, (Supervisor), Mrs M. Wild and Miss C. Smith.

Ten
People and Places

Within the five square miles which form our ancient township are the hamlets and districts of Baretrees, Busk, Butler Green, Chadderton Fold, Coalshaw Green, Cowhill, Foxdenton, Greengate, Healds Green, Hollinwood, Middleton Junction, Mills Hill, Nimble Nook, Nordens, Stockbrook, Streetbridge, Washbrook and Whitegate. A selection of views looking at some of these areas and the people who lived there, completes our story.

Chadderton Hospital, c. 1955. This isolation hospital at Racefield, on the northern boundary of the town, was originally opened in about 1878 by the Chadderton Local Board. In 1894 a joint hospital committee was formed with representatives of Chadderton, Royton and Crompton urban district councils. A new smallpox hospital was erected in 1917 at a cost of £12,000. The premises are now in use as Racefield Hamlet - a group of highly desirable residences.

Mary with James and Fred Sudworth enjoying themselves at the little playground, known locally as the 'Donkey Park', on the Park Estate, c. 1950.

The farm house at Chadderton Hall Farm in 1960. Shortly afterwards it was demolished so that the council could straighten out the length of road from St Matthew's church to Haigh Lane.

The Ashworth family pose on their allotment at the Fernhurst Mill in 1923.

A crowded Middleton Road sometime in the 1950s gives a good indication of the fashions of the period! The occasion is the annual Whit Sunday Combined Service held in the town hall gardens. The high wall, later lowered, and recently rebuilt in the same style as the town hall, surrounds the three mid-nineteenth century houses known as Rushbank.

The exterior of Parkside House prior to its demolition in August 1988. This impressive house was built in about 1860 as the home of a mill owner and was situated behind the high retaining wall on Middleton Road West. The private enclave of Packwood Chase now occupies the site.

In September 1961 work was progressing well on the realignment of Chadderton Hall Road from St Matthew's church to Haigh Lane. Prior to this, the old road now curving through the park was the main highway. The bus is from the former Oldham Corporation fleet with its livery of maroon and cream.

Tomlinson's farm house at Chadderton Hall after a particularly bad snowfall in January 1955.

One of the large houses of yesteryear was Albion House, which was home to George Herbert Wrigley, a Chadderton councillor. It stood near the junction of Broadway and Middleton Road, was later purchased by St Herbert's church, and demolished to build their present parish centre.

A view which has been much altered by 'progress' and the passing of time. This is the Broadway and Burnley Lane junction in January 1964, when plans were being made to install traffic lights at this busy crossroads. Six years later the construction of the A627(M) link road would alter this area beyond recognition as Chadderton was joined to the nation's motorway network. All the property in the picture was to go with the exception of the Elk Mill, the last mill to be built in both Chadderton and Lancashire.

The boundary of Chadderton and Oldham at Burnley Lane in the early 1970s. This section of the main road was to become relatively quiet once the Chadderton Way extension to the A627(M) was opened. The Black Cow public house was near the gable end, visible left of centre.

The construction of the A627(M) link road transformed the landscape in north Chadderton. This scene from September 1970 shows the Horton Arms, Streetbridge, behind the crane, whilst the road cuts through Chadderton Heights in the distance.

Middleton Road from its junction with Ferney Field Road, around 1910. Little is known about Park House on the left which was demolished about fifty years ago. Beyond it was the Norden's branch of the Co-op, now occupied by Video World and Fish World. The original premises of the Hunt Lane Tavern can be seen in the centre.

Looking down Middleton Road, c. 1905. The large house to the right, Holly Bank, is still in existence but Parkside House, seen in its elevated position beyond, was demolished in 1988. The houses in the left foreground stood at the junction of Ferney Field Road until their demolition in the 1960s.

A scene from early this century as the occupant of No. 89 Foxdenton Lane poses for the camera. Most of the houses in this area have now been demolished.

Foxdenton Lane, possibly in the 1940s. The four houses in the centre, Brownhill Terrace 1898, still remain but the ones to the left have gone. Also demolished are Brown Hill Farm and the Baytree Mills in the distance. The chimney to the left belonged to Junction Mill.

A dedicated worker for St Herbert's Sunday school in its early days was Miss Rosie O'Grady. Here she is seen in about 1920, passing the town hall with some of the children in her care.

One of the stalwarts on Chadderton Council was Herbert Brabin, who served from 1928 to 1946. He was twice chairman of the council, in 1931-32 and 1932-33, and was Chairman of Governors at Chadderton Grammar School in its early days.

Whilst going about their daily chores, this group of ladies from Queens Road was snapped by the photographer. The scene is sometime before the First World War.

It is the early 1920s and this very smartly dressed group pose on Prog Bridge, which crossed the canal at the Boat and Horses. Shortly afterwards, Broadway was commenced and the bridge was replaced with the modern Brierley Bridge. Recently that bridge has also been removed during the construction work on the M66 extension through Chadderton. The low buildings to the right of the public house were part of the First World War aircraft assembly plant, and later became part of the Her Majesty's Stationery Office complex.

Milne Street, c. 1970, from its junction with Middleton Road. The ornate building was the original Reform Club, opened in the 1890s, and upstairs was the Free Trade Hall which eventually served as the Lyric cinema. The waste land behind - the site of the Wren Mill - was being prepared for building the first Asda superstore.

Butler Green under redevelopment in the 1970s. The building to the left was formerly Butler Green Police Station and is now used as a hostel. The property to the right of centre stood at the junction of Fields New Road. The area in the foreground is now set out as a public open space.

History was made in June 1970 when Chadderton's first tower blocks, Stockfield Mount and Lansdowne Court, were opened at Cowhill (later renamed Crossley!)

The official opening of the North Western Electricity Board's new offices off Middleton Road is recalled in this scene. This was in September 1966 and the building, much altered, is now the Chadderton Total Care rest home.

The famous clock tower on the Methodist church at Washbrook has gone, and in its place a new parade of shops arises. The was the scene in February 1974.

Old Lane as it appeared in September 1961. Only the Colliers Arms, which dates back to the early nineteenth century remains, and even this has been greatly altered. The road in the right foreground is Chadderton's little known 'Union' Street!

The Halford Pavilion in Coalshaw Green Park shortly after its opening in 1969. The park itself was opened in 1911 as a gift from the Lees family of Werneth Park.

The Butler Green and Washbrook crossroads in December 1964. The lorry turning from Coalshaw Green Road belonged to the park's department and was painted in the red livery of Chadderton Council. Shortly afterwards the council changed over to a yellow livery.

A landmark at Butler Green is the railway bridge on Stanley Road. The line was opened in 1880 with a station at Hollinwood, in south east Chadderton. The famous clock tower of the Methodist church can be seen through the arch.

This strange house known as Drury Castle was on Drury Lane. These views from 1942 show the weird and wonderful collection of carvings which adorned the property.

The architectural oddity came about as a result of a disagreement between neighbours. One of them, Bill Lees, put a window in the side of his house overlooking the home of Edward Whittaker, a millwright. The latter then built the wall which incorporated all these stone figures, collected from far and near.

Mr James Crossley Smith and his wife Hannah Maria (née Wolstencroft). He was one of the two members of the Independent Labour Party who contested South Ward in the first election for the Chadderton UDC in 1894. Although defeated on that occasion, he was elected unopposed in 1901 and was to serve continuously on the council until 1914, being its chairman in 1907-8.

A busy Whitsuntide scene at Butler Green in the 1930s. This was quite a substantial village until redevelopment took place in the 1970s. A cluster of shops stood at the crossroads whilst Washbrook Methodist church, with its public clock, formed the focal point for the community.

Mr Llewellyn Patch stands with a customer at the door of his chemists shop at Butler Green in the 1930s. Judging from the window displays, he sold a wide variety of goods including 'cement' for repairing nylon stockings!

A charming Edwardian photograph from about 1906, of the Smith family who lived at Mary's Mind, a house near the canal bridge on Henshaw Lane. John, who was the manager at the nearby Bower Colliery, is seen with his wife, Mary, and is holding baby Charlotte. The other children are, from left to right: Thomas, Emma, Richard and Hannah. The couple later had three more children - Mary, and twins William and John. Charlotte outlived them all and died in 1996.

The corner of Bower Lane and Henshaw Lane early this century. The area is now altered beyond recognition with motorway and retail development.

Duckworth's corner shop at Butler Green. A notice to the left of the youth's head reads: 'Police Notice. Lost - a Gold 9ct Bangle'.

The Rose Queen and retinue from Butler Green Mission passing the Britannia Hotel at Washbrook, c. 1951.

Congregations of the churches in the south Chadderton area come together at the junction of Thompson Lane, Eaves Lane and Whitegate Lane, for their joint service in about 1930. All this terraced property is still with us. A single deck bus was used to get under the low railway bridges on this route to Middleton Junction.

This branch of the Co-operative Society was at the junction of Long Lane and Broadway. The displays of tinned food, joints of meat and patent medicines in this 1937 view, have now given way to a store supplying the needs of the modern motorist.